SPIRALIZER COOKBOOK

60 Best Delicious & Healthy Spiralizer Recipes You Have to Try!

MARK EVANS

© **Copyright 2017 by Mark Evans - All rights reserved.**

The following Book is reproduced below with the goal of providing information that is as accurate and as reliable as possible. Regardless, purchasing this Book can be seen as consent to the fact that both the publisher and the author of this book are in no way experts on the topics discussed within, and that any recommendations or suggestions made herein are for entertainment purposes only. Professionals should be consulted as needed before undertaking any of the action endorsed herein.

This declaration is deemed fair and valid by both the American Bar Association and the Committee of Publishers Association and is legally binding throughout the United States.

Furthermore, the transmission, duplication or reproduction of any of the following work, including precise information, will be considered an illegal act, irrespective whether it is done electronically or in print. The legality extends to creating a secondary or tertiary copy of the work or a recorded copy and is only allowed with express written consent of the Publisher. All additional rights are reserved.

The information in the following pages is broadly considered to be a truthful and accurate account of facts, and as such any inattention, use or misuse of the information in question by the reader will render any resulting actions solely under their purview. There are no scenarios in which the publisher or the original author of this work can be in any fashion deemed liable for any hardship or damages that may befall them after undertaking information described herein.

Additionally, the information found on the following pages is intended for informational purposes only and should thus be considered, universal. As befitting its nature, the information presented is without assurance regarding its continued validity or interim quality. Trademarks that mentioned are done without written consent and can in no way be considered an endorsement from the trademark holder.

Table of Contents

Introduction 1

Chapter 1 – The Spiralizer and Why You Need One 3

Chapter 2 – Breakfast Spiralizer Recipes 10

Recipe #1 – Oatmeal with Apple Cinnamon 10

Recipe #2 - Carrot Fritters 12

Recipe #3 –Carrot Zoodles and Coconut Crostino 14

Recipe #4: Banana Hotcakes 16

Recipe #5 – Cucumber Carrot Salad 18

Recipe #6 - Plantain Fries 20

Recipe #7 - Carrot Rice Salad 22

Recipe #8 – Apples with Peanut Butter Sauce 24

Recipe #9 - Zucchini Salad 26

Recipe #10 - Zucchini Rice with Cider Dressing 28

Recipe #11 - Sweet Potato Bake 30

Recipe #12 - Apple and Rhubarb Crisp 32

Recipe #13 - Turnip Noodle Soup 34

Recipe #14 - Apple and Pear Matches with Sugar-Cinnamon Mix 36

Recipe #15 - Sweet Potato Curls 38

Chapter 3 – Spiralizer Lunch Menus 40

Recipe #16 - Cucumber, Zucchini, and Jicama Salad 40

Recipe #17 - Spiced Sweet Potato Noodle Soup 43

Recipe #18 - Red Rice with Nuts and Cheese 45

Recipe #19 - Squash with Chicken Tikka Masala 47

Recipe #20 - Cold Watermelon Soup with Chunky Beet 50

Recipe #21 - Collard Green Wrap 52

Recipe #22 – Pesto Zucchini Noodles 54

Recipe #23 - Chilled Cucumber Noodles 56

Recipe #24 - Tuna Veggie Casserole 58

Recipe #25 - Spiced Carrot Rice Bowl 60

Recipe #26 - Rainbow Seafood Marinara 62

Recipe #27: Italian Meatball Stew with Zucchini Noodles 66

Recipe #28 – Summer Broccoli and Carrots Slaw 69

Recipe #29 - Carrot Rice and Lentil Stew 71

Recipe #30 – Spiralized Turnip Risotto with Broccoli Pesto 73

Chapter 4 – Spiralizer Dinner Options 75

Recipe #31 –Egg Drop Soup 75

Recipe #32 - Carrot Noodles in Miso 77

Recipe #33 - Herb Carrot Rice 79

Recipe #34 - Chicken Zucchini Noodles 81

Recipe #35 - Stir Fry Broccoli Zoodles and Beef Steak 83

Recipe #36 - Mediterranean Zoodle Platter 86

Recipe #37 - Beet Noodles with Mustard Glaze 88

Recipe #38 - Beet Rice Wrap with Pesto Sauce 90

Recipe #39 - Beets and Beans Pickles 93

Recipe #40 - Curly Sweet Potato Fries 95

Recipe #41 - Sweet Potato Noodles with Kale Pesto 97

Recipe #42 - Sweet Potato Wraps 99

Recipe #43 – Shredded Cabbage Bowl 101

Recipe #44 - Butternut Squash and Spinach Casserole 103

Recipe#45 - Stir-Fry Radish Zoodles and Mushrooms . 106

Chapter 5 – Pasta and Salad Dishes 108

Recipe#46 - Radish, Beetroot, and Carrot Zoodles 108

Recipe #47 – Spiralized Rutabaga Pasta with Marinara Sauce 111

Recipe #48 - Green and Yellow Mango Salad 113

Recipe #49 – Sweet Potatoes and Prosciutto Pasta 115

Recipe #50 - Beet Caprese Pasta 117

Recipe #51 - Cucumber Pasta in White Sauce 119

Recipe #52 - Zucchini Lasagna 121

Recipe #53 – Quinoa Beets Salad 124

Recipe #54 - Parsnip Puttanesca 126

Recipe #55 - Sausage Salad with Cucumber and Zucchini Zoodles 128

Recipe #56 – Spiralized Apples Salad 130

Recipe #57 - Beet Pasta with Pumpkin Sauce 132

Recipe #58 - Zucchini Pasta with Baked Meatballs 135

Recipe #59 – Carbonara Zoodles 137

Recipe #60 - Zucchini Ribbons Salad 139
Conclusion **141**

Introduction

I would like to thank and congratulate you for purchasing the book "Spiralizer - 60 Best Delicious & Healthy Spiralizer Recipes You Have to Try!"

This book contains proven steps and strategies on how to use your spiralizer for many different kinds of dishes. If you are trying to find healthier alternatives to your regular pasta dishes and add in more vegetables into your diet, then this book is for you.

This book contains 60 delicious and healthy spiralizer recipes that would really make the most out of your spiralizer. The recipes are not only healthy but are also easy to follow. If you are new to this kind of appliance, the first part of the book will help you get more information as to how it is properly used.

Spiralizing vegetables and fruits is also a great way of customizing your recipes and transforming them to a healthier and more nutrient-rich food. By the time you finish reading this book, you will have more ideas of recreating healthier versions of your favorite meals using the spiralizer.

Get to know more about the spiralizer and how it can positively affect your kitchen activities for an even easier and faster food prepping!

Thanks again for purchasing this book. I hope you enjoy it!

Chapter 1 - The Spiralizer and Why You Need One

Spiralizing is a method of transforming vegetables and fruits such as cucumbers, carrots, zucchinis, apples, and sweet potatoes among others into noodles, ribbons, pasta or thin vegetable strips. Did you know that you can even make rice out of a spiralized vegetable? All you have to do is place the veggie of choice in a food processor and chop into smaller bits.

The technique makes cutting fruits and vegetables a lot easier thereby minimizing time in the kitchen. But to become successful at spiralizing, you will need to purchase a durable spiralizer that is easy to use, assemble, and clean.

Ever since the introduction of spiralizers on the market, it has become a kitchen essential. A spiralizer is a kind of machine that can slice hardy veggies and fruits into noodle strands. If you wanted a healthier substitute for wheat-based noodles, it is possible to have these zoodles as an alternative.

Benefits of Spiralizing

The spiralizer helps create clean-flavored meals that look mouth-watering but won't add up to the weighing scale. Some of the benefits of eating spiralized fruits and vegetables include the following:

- Spiralizing helps you consume more fruits and vegetables - most of the recipes found in this book are primarily veggie-friendly with small amounts of protein, lean meat, and dairy. If you wanted to shift to a healthier diet, having a spiralizer will help you transition to an organic lifestyle.

- Spiralizing helps you lose weight – since you are mostly going to use fresh produce, you are sure that you will get a good amount of vital nutrients that consist of fiber, protein, good carbs, and minerals found in fruits and vegetables. It also helps that zoodles are low in calories, salt, and sugar.

- Spiralizing makes it easier for you to follow a strict diet – whether you are on a Paleo, Pescatarian, Vegetarian, or vegan diet, spiralizing helps you prepare noodles and vegetable strips that stick to the strict guidelines of the abovementioned diets.

- Spiralizing helps you not to miss out on your favorite pasta dishes - Zoodles are not only gluten-free, but they also cook faster than your ordinary pasta because for one, they are lightly cooked, and two, they are best served raw and fresh.

- Spiralizing helps you experiment on different fruits and veggies - If you are looking for variety, then this kitchen appliance is for you. With the spiralizer, you can let your creativity flow in the kitchen.

- Spiralizing makes meals look more tempting and scrumptious – spiralizing makes dishes that are pleasing to the eye. Since you will deal mostly with veggies, you forgo of the typical chopped, diced, or julienned veggies. This technique improves food presentation, which subsequently intensifies one's appetite for organic food.

- The spiralizer does not run on electricity – you need not worry about your electric bill consumption adding up to your monthly bills.

- The spiralizer helps keep your health in check –You get to incorporate more fruits and vegetables into your daily meals. The moment you get used to using your spiralizer, you will want to use it for almost every meal. You gradually get used to eating fresh and healthy. This is especially beneficial if you are cooking for kids.

Popular Food that Can Be Spiralized

Here are some of the food that you can make with the help of a Spiralizer:

- Noodles
- Spaghetti
- Vegetable rice
- Pickled vegetables

- Salads
- Soups and stews
- Waffles
- One-pot meals
- Omelets
- Fries
- Desserts

Just have fun while cooking and get more creative with your ingredients. With a Spiralizer in the kitchen, the possibilities are endless.

How to Use the Spiralizer

The following is a step-by-step process of spiralizing fruits and vegetables:

Step 1 - Place the Spiralizer to the countertop or a specific spot in the kitchen where it can't be moved or tippled over. A place where it will just be steady and unmovable.

Step 2 – Pick a specific fruit or vegetable you wish to spiralize. You may either peel the skin or keep it intact. Just make sure to flatten the sides of the vegetable before spiralizing.

Step 3 - Push one side of the vegetable on the blade. Center the vegetable to get uniform result.

Step 4 - Push the sharp side of the spiralizer towards the other side of the vegetable/fruit. Keep the veggie secure so it won't easily fall off once the process of spiralizing is going on.

Step 5 – Put a bowl underneath the blades to catch the zoodles. Turn the handle clockwise and wait for the noodles to come out.

Step 6 – If the strands seem too long for you, you can trim the noodles into shorter strands using a pair of scissors or a kitchen knife to cut the strands into smaller pieces.

Note: You can spiralize almost all types of fruits and vegetables, but most of the common ones are potatoes, sweet potatoes, zucchinis, apples, carrots, beets, broccoli, squash, cabbage, turnip, and radish among others.

Spiralizer Blades

Blade A - This has a straight blade and has the widest of all the blades. This kind of blade makes long, flat zoodles, ribbons, chips from potatoes, apples, and sweet potatoes, and bigger slices of veggies.

Blade B - This has triangular blades that make spaghetti-like noodles, but are a little thicker than the regular ones. Some of the veggies that make the best noodles are potato, cucumber, and zucchini.

Blade C - This has smaller triangular blades that make noodles a tad thicker than angel hair pasta. Thin zoodles are perfect for pasta dishes with little or no sauces, and for salads as well.

Chapter 2 – Breakfast Spiralizer Recipes

Recipe #1 – Oatmeal with Apple Cinnamon

Prep time – 10 minutes
Serving size – 1

Nutrition facts:
Calories – 160
Carbohydrates – 33 grams
Total Fat – 2 grams
Protein – 4 grams

Ingredients:
- 1 medium apple, whole
- 1 Tbsp. roasted cashews, lightly salted
- 1 Tbsp. raisins
- ½ cup steel-cut oats
- 1 cup milk
- 1 tbsp. honey
- Dash of cinnamon powder

- Dash of nutmeg
- Drop of vanilla extract

Directions:
1. Pour in oats and milk in a saucepan. Stir and wait for the mixture to boil.
2. Reduce the heat and cook for 5 minutes whilst stirring often. Once the oats thicken, remove from the saucepan and set aside.
3. Sprinkle cinnamon powder, nutmeg powder, and vanilla extract over the oats. Stir well.
4. Using Blade A of the spiralizer, slice the whole apple into disks. Toss into the oats.
5. Put raisings and cashew nuts on top. Drizzle in honey. Serve warm.

Recipe #2 - Carrot Fritters

Prep time – 30 minutes
Serving size – 5

Nutrition facts:
Calories – 80.8
Carbohydrates – 4.2 grams
Total Fat – 4.5 grams
Protein – 6.0 grams

Ingredients:
- 2 large carrots, peeled
- 1 cup corn meal
- 4 scallions, chopped
- 1 teaspoon turmeric powder
- 2 eggs, whisked
- Pinch of salt, add more if needed
- Pinch of pepper, to taste
- 2 tablespoons olive oil
- 1 cup Greek yoghurt, for dipping

Directions:
1. Using Blade C of the spiralizer, spiralize carrots into thin noodles. Trim into 3 inch strands to shorten noodles.
2. Place carrot noodles, corn meal, scallions, turmeric powder, and eggs in a bowl. Season with salt and pepper.
3. Meanwhile, heat the olive oil in a pan. Pour ¼ cup of the fritter mixture onto a nonstick skillet. Cook for 3 minutes. Flip over and cook for another 2 minutes.
4. Repeat the same procedure until all fritters are cooked.
5. Serve fritters with Greek yoghurt as dipping.

Recipe #3 – Carrot Zoodles and Coconut Crostino

Prep time – 30 minutes
Serving size – 4

Nutrition facts:
Calories – 207.6
Carbohydrates – 35 grams
Total Fat – 20.1 grams
Protein – 5.2 grams

Ingredients:
- 1 medium carrot, peeled
- ½ cup ricotta cheese
- 4 slices of wheat bread, toasted
- ½ cup honey
- 1 tablespoon coconut flakes
- Pinch of sea salt, add more if needed
- Pinch of pepper, to taste

Directions:
1. Preheat the oven to 400°F. Line a baking sheet with parchment paper.

2. Using Blade C, spiralize the carrot. Trim noodles into 3-inch strands. Transfer to a baking sheet. Drizzle in maple syrup all over noodles. Season with salt and pepper.
3. Roast the noodles for 20 minutes. Flip noodles over after 10 minutes for an even roasting.
4. Top toasted bread slices with ricotta cheese. Place carrot noodles on top of each bread. Sprinkle coconut flakes and drizzle in maple syrup. Serve.

Recipe #4: Banana Hotcakes

Prep time – 15 minutes
Serving size – 2

Nutrition facts:
Calories – 246.6
Carbohydrates – 48.4 grams
Total Fat – 2.6 grams
Protein – 9.3 grams

Ingredients:
- 1 egg, lightly beaten
- ¼ tsp. baking powder
- 2 Tbsp. all-purpose flour
- ¼ cup milk
- 1 tsp. white sugar
- Drop of vanilla extract
- Dash of nutmeg
- 2 tablespoons olive oil
- 2 almost ripe bananas
- Dash of powdered sugar

Directions:

1. Pour egg, baking powder, all-purpose flour, milk, sugar, vanilla extract, and nutmeg in a bowl. Mix well. Set aside.
2. Using Blade A of the spiralizer, chop plantains into thin disks. Transfer into the batter.
3. Pour olive oil into a skillet. Swirl around to coat. Pour ½ cup of the batter into the pan. Cook the hotcake for 2 minutes on the first side and 1 minute on the other side or until bubbles form in the middle and the edges are set and.
4. Transfer the hotcakes into a serving plate. Repeat the same procedure until all the batter is cooked.
5. Stack pancakes and sprinkle with powdered sugar. Serve.

Recipe #5 – Cucumber Carrot Salad

Prep time – 45 minutes
Serving size – 4

Nutrition facts:
Calories – 65.9
Carbohydrates – 12.9 grams
Total Fat – 1.7 grams
Protein – 1.3 grams

Ingredients:
- 1 medium cucumber
- 1 carrot, peeled
- 1 cup canned chickpeas
- 1 red onion, sliced thinly
- 1 cup cherry tomato, halved
- 1 ½ tablespoon olive oil
- ½ teaspoon cumin powder
- ½ teaspoon chili powder
- 2 tablespoons lemon juice
- 1 teaspoon lemon zest
- Pinch of sea salt, add more if needed
- ¼ teaspoon ground black pepper

Directions:

1. Spiralize the cucumber and carrot using Blade C of the spiralizer. Place spiralized veggies in a bowl. Add in vegetables in chickpeas, onions, and cherry tomatoes. Set aside.
2. In a separate bowl, put together olive oil, curry powder, cumin, lemon juice, and lemon zest. Season with salt and pepper.
3. Pour the dressing over the veggies. Toss well. Place inside the fridge for 30 minutes before serving.

Recipe #6 - Plantain Fries

Prep time – 45 minutes
Serving size – 2

Nutrition facts:
Calories – 550
Carbohydrates – 0 gram
Total Fat – 0 gram
Protein – 0 gram

Ingredients:
- 2 unripe plantains
- 1 Tbsp. all-purpose flour
- 1 tsp. corn meal
- 1 egg, lightly beaten
- Pinch of sea salt, add more if needed
- olive oil to deep fry plantains

Directions:
1. Put together corn meal and all-purpose flour in a bowl. Set aside.
2. Using Blade B of the spiralizer, slice plantains into long, thick noodles

resembling that of a French Fries cut. Drop spiralized plantains into the egg.
3. Dredge fries into the flour-cornmeal mix.
4. Pour olive oil into the skillet. Place flour-coated plantains into the skillet. Cook for 3 minutes or until golden.
5. Transfer fries and drain on paper towels. Repeat the procedure until all fried are cooked.
6. Sprinkle a little sea salt over the fritters. Serve.

Recipe #7 - Carrot Rice Salad

Prep time – 30 minutes
Serving size – 4

Nutrition facts:
Calories – 84.4
Carbohydrates – 15.5 gram
Total Fat – 2.0 gram
Protein – 2.2 grams

Ingredients:
- 2 large carrots, peeled
- 1 teaspoon jalapenos, chopped
- ¼ cup vegetable broth
- 2 tablespoons pumpkin seeds, roasted
- 2 garlic cloves, minced
- 2 red bell pepper, deseeded
- 3 tomatoes, chopped
- ½ cup red onion, chopped
- 2 avocados, peeled, diced
- 3 tablespoons cilantro, chopped
- 2 tablespoons lime juice
- 1 tablespoon olive oil

Directions:

1. Spiralize carrots using Blade C of the spiralizer. Chop the noodles into a grain-like consistency. Set aside.
2. Meanwhile, mix together onion, avocado, tomatoes, cilantro, and lime juice. Stir well. Set aside.
3. Roast peppers on a grill pan. Remove the charred skin and chop the meat to small pieces. Set aside.
4. Heat the olive oil in a pan. Cook garlic, carrot rice, and jalapenos for 3 minutes. Season with salt and pepper. Pour vegetable broth. Allow the rice to simmer for 5 minutes
5. To serve, scoop rice into bowls. Add in avocado salsa and roasted peppers on top. Sprinkle pumpkin seeds. Serve.

Recipe #8 – Apples with Peanut Butter Sauce

Prep time – 20 minutes
Serving size – 1

Nutrition facts:
Calories – 178.6
Carbohydrates – 30.1 grams
Total Fat – 4.6 grams
Protein – 6.6 grams

Ingredients:
For the sauce
- 2 Tbsp. milk
- ¼ tsp. nutmeg powder
- 2 Tbsp. peanut butter

For the apple crisps
- 1 apple, sliced into thin disks
- 2 Tbsp. raw pecans
- ½ lemon juice, freshly squeezed
- 2 Tbsp. dry coconut flakes, sweet
- Drizzle of pure maple syrup

Directions:

1. For the sauce, combine nutmeg powder, milk, and peanut butter in a bowl. Stir until all ingredients are well incorporated. Set aside.
2. For the apple, brown pecans in a skillet for 5 minutes or until fragrant. Set aside to cool. Once cooled to touch, chop pecans.
3. In the same skillet, toast coconut flakes for 4 minutes or until golden brown. Set aside.
4. Using Blade A of the spiralizer, spiralize apple disks. Drizzle in lemon juice to prevent from browning.
5. Place apples on a serving plate. Drizzle in with nutmeg and peanut butter mixture.
6. Top toasted coconut flakes, chopped pecans, and maple syrup. Serve.

Recipe #9 - Zucchini Salad

Prep time – 45 minutes
Serving size – 5 - 6

Nutrition facts:
Calories – 76
Carbohydrates – 10.5 grams
Total Fat – 3.8 grams
Protein – 1.8 grams

Ingredients:
- 1 tablespoon balsamic vinegar
- ½ teaspoon Dijon mustard
- 1 tablespoon olive oil
- 1 tablespoon honey
- 2 zucchinis
- 5 cups kale leaves, chopped
- 2 cups lettuce leaves, chopped
- 1 green apple, diced
- Pinch of sea salt, add more if needed

Directions:

1. Put together balsamic vinegar, mustard, olive oil, honey, and sea salt in a bowl. Set aside.
2. Using Blade A of the spiralizer, spiralize zucchinis into ribbons. Transfer to a salad bowl. Add in apples, kale, and lettuce.
3. Pour just the right amount of vinaigrette. Toss well to combine.
4. Chill the salad for 1 hour before serving.

Recipe #10 - Zucchini Rice with Cider Dressing

Prep time – 30 minutes
Serving size – 4

Nutrition facts:
Calories – 259
Carbohydrates – 61.4 grams
Total Fat – 168 grams
Protein – 29.5 grams

Ingredients:
- 2 large zucchinis
- 4 strips bacon
- 1 teaspoon mustard
- 1 tablespoon maple syrup
- ½ tablespoon olive oil
- 1 ½ tablespoon apple cider vinegar
- 2 tablespoons raisins
- ¾ cup almonds, chopped
- ½ cup dried apricots, chopped
- ½ cup cottage cheese
- Pinch of sea salt, add more if needed

- Pinch of pepper, to taste

Directions:
1. Using Blade C of the spiralizer, spiralize zucchini into thin noodles. Place on a chopping board and then chop zoodles into grain-like pieces. Set aside.
2. Meanwhile, cook bacon strips in a pan for 7 minutes or until crisp. Transfer to a chopping and mince cooked bacon. Set aside.
3. Whisk together mustard, maple syrup, olive oil, and apple cider vinegar in a bowl. Set aside until ready to use.
4. To assemble, zucchini rice, raisins, almonds, apricots, and cottage cheese in a bowl. Pour just the right amount of vinaigrette. Season with salt and pepper. Toss well to combine. Garnish with minced bacon on top.

RECIPE #11 - SWEET POTATO BAKE

Prep time – 30 minutes
Serving size – 4

Nutrition facts:
Calories – 103.7
Carbohydrates – 15.9 grams
Total Fat – 4.1 grams
Protein – 1.1 grams

Ingredients:
- 1 sweet potato, peeled
- 1 tablespoon olive oil
- 1 ½ cup tomatoes, diced
- ½ cup onions, chopped
- 1 tablespoon garlic, minced
- 5 eggs
- 1 tablespoon cilantro, chopped
- ¼ teaspoon cumin
- ¼ teaspoon paprika
- 1 jalapeno pepper, chopped
- Pinch of sea salt, add more if needed
- Pinch of pepper, to taste

Directions:

1. Preheat the oven to 350°F. Lightly grease 4 ramekins with oil.
2. Using Blade C of the spiralizer, spiralize sweet potato. Trim noodles into long strands.
3. Meanwhile, heat the oil in a pan. Sauté garlic, onions, and jalapeno for 3 minutes.
4. Add sweet potato noodles, tomatoes, paprika, cumin, salt and pepper. Cook for 7 minutes or until the juices thicken.
5. Transfer sweet potato into the ramekins. Break an egg on top of each ramekin. Bake for 10 minutes. Garnish with cilantro. Serve.

Recipe #12 - Apple and Rhubarb Crisp

Prep time – 40 minutes
Serving size – 3

Nutrition facts:
Calories – 307.2
Carbohydrates – 40.6 grams
Total Fat – 50.7 grams
Protein – 2.6 grams

Ingredients:
- 3 apples
- 4 rhubarb stalks, diced
- 1 cup granola
- 4 teaspoons maple syrup

Directions:
1. Preheat the oven to 375°F. Prepare 3 ramekins.
2. Using Blade C of the spiralizer, spiralize apples to create strands. Transfer apple noodles in a bowl. Add in rhubarb. Toss well to combine.

3. Spoon apple rhubarb mixture into each ramekins. Drizzle in maple syrup into each ramekin. Place inside the oven and bake for 20 minutes.
4. Spoon granola on top of each ramekin. Bake for another 5 minutes. Serve.

Recipe #13 - Turnip Noodle Soup

Prep time – 45 minutes
Serving size – 4

Nutrition facts:
Calories – 102.5
Carbohydrates – 13.0 grams
Total Fat – 3.0 grams
Protein – 7.6 grams

Ingredients:
- 1 turnip, edges peeled
- 2 chicken breast halves, boiled, diced
- 2 carrots, diced
- 1 onion, chopped
- 2 celery stalks, chopped
- 3 garlic cloves, minced
- 4 cups chicken stock
- 1 tablespoon thyme leaves, chopped
- 2 tablespoons butter, unsalted
- Pinch of sea salt, add more if needed
- Pinch of ground black pepper, to taste

Directions:
1. Grease the sides and bottom of a pot with butter. Layer the chicken breast, onions, carrots, and celery. Cover and cook for 10 minutes.
2. Add in thyme. Season with salt and pepper. Pour the chicken stock. Allow to simmer for 20 minutes.
3. Meanwhile, using Blade B of the spiralizer, spiralize turnip into noodles.
4. Add in turnip noodles into the chicken soup. Bring to a boil. Reduce the heat and allow to simmer for 5 minutes. Serve hot.

Recipe #14 - Apple and Pear Matches with Sugar-Cinnamon Mix

Prep time – 20 minutes
Serving size – 2

Nutrition facts:
Calories – 134
Carbohydrates – 21.0 grams
Total Fat – 5.4 grams
Protein – 3.4 grams

Ingredients:
- 1 apple, whole
- 1 pear, whole
- ¾ cup tapioca flour
- ½ cup olive oil
- 1 Tbsp. cinnamon powder
- ½ cup brown sugar

Directions:
1. Combine cinnamon powder and brown sugar in a bowl. Set aside.

2. Using Blade B of the spiralizer, slice apple and pear into thin sticks. Slice the sticks into smaller lengths as that of a matchstick.
3. Dredge into the tapioca flour to prevent from browning.
4. Heat the olive oil in a skillet. Carefully slide into the pan with hot oil. Fry for 3 minutes or until golden brown. Drain on paper towels.
5. To serve, arrange fruit matches on a platter. Sprinkle with cinnamon-sugar mixture. Serve.

Recipe #15 - Sweet Potato Curls

Prep time – 30 minutes
Serving size – 4

Nutrition facts:
Calories – 160
Carbohydrates – 14.0 grams
Total Fat – 11.0 grams
Protein – 1.0 gram

Ingredients:
- 2 sweet potatoes, peeled
- 1 tablespoon almond flour
- ½ cup almond milk
- 2 tablespoons butter, divided
- ½ cup cheddar cheese, grated
- ½ cup Parmesan cheese, grated
- 2 tablespoons parsley, chopped

Directions:
1. Use Blade B of the spiralizer, spiralize the sweet potatoes to thin noodles. Trim noodles into curls. Set aside.

2. Meanwhile, melt half the butter in a skillet. Pour spiralized sweet potato curls. Cook for 10 minutes. Set aside.
3. In the same pan, melt the remaining butter. Add in almond flour. Mix well to form a roux. Pour milk and mix until it thickens.
4. Add sweet potato curls. Stir well. Sprinkle Parmesan and cheddar cheese. Cook until the cheese melts.
5. To serve, place dish on a platter. Garnish with parsley.

Chapter 3 – Spiralizer Lunch Menus

Recipe #16 - Cucumber, Zucchini, and Jicama Salad

Prep time – 30 minutes
Serving size – 4

Nutrition facts:
Calories – 98.6
Carbohydrates – 4.8 grams
Total Fat – 8.7 grams
Protein – 0.8 gram

Ingredients:

For the dressing
- 2 Tbsp. mayonnaise
- 1 can tuna chunks in brine, drained
- ½ cup Greek yogurt, plain
- ¼ tsp. garlic powder
- 2 eggs, soft-boiled, roughly chopped
- 1 celery stalks, minced

- ¼ tsp. sea salt
- Pinch of black pepper

For the salad
- 1 zucchini, unpeeled
- 1 cucumber, unpeeled
- ¼ jicama, peeled

*All must be chilled before use

Directions:
1. For the dressing, combine mayonnaise, tuna chunks, Greek yogurt, garlic powder, eggs, celery stalks, salt, and pepper into a bowl. Mix until all ingredients are well incorporated. Place inside the fridge for 30 minutes.
2. For the salad, Using Blade B of the spiralizer, spiralize cucumber into thick noodles.
3. Using Blade A of the spiralizer, spiralize jicama into flat noodles.
4. Using Blade C of the spiralizer, spiralize zucchini into thin noodles.

5. To serve, put together all zoodles in a salad bowl. Pour just the right amount of dressing all over spiralized veggies. Toss to combine. Serve.

Recipe #17 - Spiced Sweet Potato Noodle Soup

Prep time – 30 minutes
Serving size – 2

Nutrition facts:
Calories – 296
Carbohydrates – 27.2 grams
Total Fat – 15.2 grams
Protein – 12.0 grams

Ingredients:
- 1 large sweet potato, peeled
- 2 cups tomatoes, diced
- 1 cup avocadoes, diced
- 3 cups vegetable stock
- ½ cup white onions, chopped
- 2 garlic cloves, minced
- ½ teaspoon cumin
- 1 tablespoon olive oil
- 1 tablespoon chili powder
- 1 tablespoon cilantro, chopped

Directions:

1. Using blade C of the spiralizer, spiralize sweet potato into long strands. Set aside.
2. Meanwhile, heat the olive oil in a large saucepan. Saute onion and garlic for 3 minutes or until translucent and fragrant.
3. Add in tomatoes. Season with salt, pepper, chili powder, and cumin. Stir well and cook for 3 minutes.
6. Pour vegetable stock into the saucepan. Once boiling, add in zoodles. Reduce the heat and allow to simmer for 7 minutes.
7. To serve, ladle an equal amount of soup into bowls. Garnish with avocado and cilantro on top.

Recipe #18 - Red Rice with Nuts and Cheese

Prep time – 30 minutes
Serving size – 2

Nutrition facts:
Calories – 180
Carbohydrates – 48.0 grams
Total Fat – 0.5 grams
Protein – 8.0 grams

Ingredients:
- 2 beets, peeled
- 1 teaspoon fresh thyme leaves
- ½ cup hazelnuts, toasted, finely chopped
- ¼ cup water
- 1 garlic clove, crushed
- 2 tablespoons onions, chopped
- 1 tablespoon olive oil
- ¼ cup Parmesan cheese, grated
- Pinch of salt, add more if needed
- Pinch of ground black pepper

Directions:
1. Using Blade C of the spiralizer, spiralize beets to create long noodles. Transfer beet noodles into a food processor. Process until grain-like consistency is achieved. Set aside.
2. Meanwhile, heat the olive oil in a pan. Sauté onion and garlic for 3 minutes then add in the beet rice and thyme leaves. Season with salt and pepper. Pour water and cook for 7 minutes whilst stirring continuously.
3. Sprinkle Parmesan cheese and hazelnuts on top of the dish. Serve on a bed of rice.

Recipe #19 - Squash with Chicken Tikka Masala

Prep time – 30 minutes
Serving size – 3

Nutrition facts:
Calories – 369.4
Carbohydrates – 25.7 grams
Total Fat – 6.3 grams
Protein – 52.8 grams

Ingredients:
- 1 butternut squash, halved
- ½ tsp. garlic powder
- Pinch of salt, add more if needed
- Pinch of white pepper, to taste

For the sauce
- 2½ Tbsp. olive oil, divided
- 1 pound chicken thigh fillets, diced
- 2 onions, minced
- 2 garlic cloves, minced
- 1 Tbsp. ginger, grated

- 1½ Tbsp. garam masala
- 1½ tsp. coriander powder
- ½ tsp. turmeric powder
- 2 tsp. cumin powder
- ¼ tsp. cayenne pepper powder
- 1 Tbsp. fresh lemon juice
- 1½ cups tomato puree
- ¼ cup Greek yogurt, plain
- 8 stalks fresh cilantro, chopped, for garnish

Directions:
1. Preheat the oven to 400°F. Line a baking sheet with parchment paper.
2. For the noodles, using Blade B of the spiralizer, spiralize the squash into thick zoodles.
3. Place on a baking sheet. Drizzle in a tablespoon of olive oil. Season with salt, pepper, and garlic powder.
4. Bake for 8 minutes or until the zoodles is fork tender. Remove the baking sheet out of the oven. Set aside.
5. For the chicken masala sauce, pour olive oil in a saucepan. Tip in diced chicken. Brown

chicken for 4 minutes or until lightly seared. Transfer to a bowl. Set aside.
6. In the same saucepan, pour in remaining oil. Sauté onion, garlic and ginger for 3 minutes or until translucent and fragrant.
7. Add in garam masala, coriander, turmeric powder, cumin, and cayenne pepper. Stir in tomato puree. Bring the mixture to a boil.
8. Reduce the heat. Add the chicken and cook for 20 minutes or until tender.
9. Remove from heat. Squeeze in lemon juice and put a dollop of yogurt.
10. To serve, put an equal amount of zoodles on a plate. Put chicken tikka masala on top. Garnish with cilantro.

Recipe #20 - Cold Watermelon Soup with Chunky Beet

Prep time – 30 minutes
Serving size – 4

Nutrition facts:
Calories – 74
Carbohydrates – 14 grams
Total Fat – 2 grams
Protein – 1 gram

Ingredients:
- 1 red onion, chopped
- ½ cucumber, diced
- 4 cups watermelon, chopped
- ½ cup tomato puree
- 1 tablespoon red-wine vinegar
- 1 tablespoon apple cider vinegar
- ½ jalapeno, chopped
- 2 tablespoons lime juice
- ½ cup basil, chopped
- 1 tablespoon olive oil
- Pinch of sea salt, add more if needed

- Pinch of pepper, to taste
- 2 beets, peeled

Directions:

1. Using a blender, put together onion, cucumber, watermelon, tomato puree, red-wine and apple cider vinegar, jalapeno, lime juice, basil, and olive oil. Pulse for 1 minute. Season with salt and pepper.
2. Pour soup in an air tight container. Place inside the fridge for 1 hour to cool before use.
3. Meanwhile, using Blade C of the spiralizer, spiralize beets. Set aside.
4. To serve, pour cold soup in individual bowls. Put an equal amount of beet noodles on top.

Recipe #21 - Collard Green Wrap

Prep time – 30 minutes
Serving size – 5

Nutrition facts:
Calories – 249.8
Carbohydrates – 22.0 grams
Total Fat – 17.0 grams
Protein – 7.6 grams

Ingredients:
- 1 cucumber
- 1 large zucchini
- 1 garlic clove, crushed
- 1 teaspoon ginger, grated
- 1 teaspoon honey
- ½ cup almond butter
- ½ cup lettuce, shredded
- 2 tablespoons coconut aminos
- 1 ½ tablespoon lemon juice
- 2 tablespoons water
- 4 large collard green leaves
- ¼ cup cilantro leaves

- 1 bell pepper, thinly sliced

Directions:

1. Using Blade C of the spiralizer, spiralize cucumber and zucchini. Trim zoodles into 2-inch strands. Set aside.
2. Meanwhile, in a blender, place garlic, ginger, honey, almond butter, coconut aminos, lemon juice, and water. Pulse mixture until smooth. Pour nut sauce in a bowl. Set aside.
3. Spread a spoonful of nut butter on the collard green leaf. Layer zucchini noodles, lettuce, cucumber noodles, cilantro, and bell pepper on top of the nut sauce. Roll collard leaf similar to that of a burrito. Do so with the remaining collard leaves.
4. Slice vegetable wraps into two. Drizzle in remaining peanut sauce.

Recipe #22 – Pesto Zucchini Noodles

Prep time – 15 minutes
Serving size – 3

Nutrition facts:
Calories – 292.7
Carbohydrates – 29.5 grams
Total Fat – 16.2 grams
Protein – 8.8 grams

Ingredients:
- 2 zucchinis
- 1 cup cherry tomatoes, halved
- 1 cup button mushrooms, halved
- 2 cups fresh basil leaves
- ¼ cup extra virgin olive oil
- 1 tablespoon butter, unsweetened
- 1 garlic clove
- Pinch of sea salt, add more if needed
- 1 teaspoon lime juice
- ¼ cup pine nuts, toasted
- ¼ teaspoon red pepper flakes

Directions:
1. Using Blade B of the spiralizer, spiralize zucchinis. Place zoodles in a microwave safe dish. Heat in the microwave for 2 minutes. Drain excess liquid. Set aside.
2. Meanwhile, in a blender, combine garlic, pine nuts, butter, lime juice. Pulse 2 time and then pour olive oil. Process for 30 seconds or until a desired consistency is achieved.
3. To serve, place zoodles, mushrooms, tomatoes, and pesto sauce. Toss well to combine.

Recipe #23 - Chilled Cucumber Noodles

Prep time – 15 minutes
Serving size – 2

Nutrition facts:
Calories – 95
Carbohydrates – 6.7 grams
Total Fat – 7.0 grams
Protein – 2.3 grams

Ingredients:

For the dressing
- 1 garlic clove, grated
- 1 can tomatoes, chopped, drained
- 2 Tbsp. fresh lemon juice
- 4 largefresh basil leaves, chopped
- ¼ tsp. lemon zest
- 2 Tbsp. extra virgin olive oil
- Pinch of sea salt, add more if needed
- Pinch of white pepper, to taste

For the salad

- 2 cucumbers, ends removed
- 1 cup arugula
- 1 cup ripe cherry tomatoes, quartered
- 4 slices feta cheese, torn
- 6 quail eggs, hard-boiled, halved

Directions:
1. For the dressing, combine garlic, tomatoes, lemon juice, basil leaves, lemon zest, olive oil, salt, and pepper in a bowl. Place inside the fridge for 15 minutes.
2. To make the salad, using Blade B of the spiralizer, spiralize cucumbers into thick zoodles. Add in arugula, cherry tomatoes, and feta cheese into a salad bowl.
3. To serve, drizzle in salad with the chilled dressing. Toss well to combine. Scatter quail eggs on top.

Recipe #24 - Tuna Veggie Casserole

Prep time – 50 minutes

Serving size – 4

Nutrition facts:

Calories – 359

Carbohydrates – 42 grams

Total Fat – 12 grams

Protein – 42 grams

Ingredients:
- 3 zucchinis
- 2 tablespoons olive oil
- ½ white onion, chopped
- 2 cups button mushrooms, halved
- 1 cup coconut milk
- 2 cups Parmesan cheese, grated
- 2 cans tuna chunks in water
- 2 teaspoons parsley, chopped
- Pinch of salt, add more if needed
- Pinch of white pepper, to taste

Directions:

1. Preheat the oven to 375°F. Prepare a baking dish.
2. Meanwhile, using Blade C of the spiralizer, spiralize zucchini. Set noodles aside.
3. Heat olive oil in a pan. Sauté onions and mushrooms for 3 minutes or until the onions are translucent and mushrooms are lightly seared.
4. Pour coconut milk into the pan. Add in tuna flakes and parsley. Season with salt and pepper. Cook for 2 minutes. Sprinkle 1 cup of Parmesan cheese. Turn off the heat.
5. Put zucchini noodles into a sauce. Stir until the zoodles are well-coated.
6. Transfer to a baking dish. Scatter remaining Parmesan cheese on top. Cover the baking dish with foil and bake for 40 minutes.

Recipe #25 - Spiced Carrot Rice Bowl

Prep time – 30 minutes
Serving size – 4

Nutrition facts:
Calories – 84.4
Carbohydrates – 15.5 grams
Total Fat – 2.0 grams
Protein – 2.2 grams

Ingredients:
- 1 large carrot, peeled
- 1 tablespoon olive oil
- ½ cup Italian sausage, sliced
- 3 teaspoons jalapeno peppers, chopped
- ½ teaspoon chili powder
- ½ cup chicken stock
- 1 tablespoon lime juice, freshly squeezed
- 1 tablespoon cilantro, chopped
- Pinch of sea salt, add more if needed
- Pinch ground black pepper, to taste
- ½ avocado, pitted, sliced

Directions:

1. Using Blade C of the spiralizer, spiralize carrots into long noodles. Transfer to a blender and pulse until a grain-like consistency is achieved. Set aside.
2. Meanwhile, heat the olive oil in a pan. Cook Italian sausage and brown for 3 minutes. Add in carrot rice, jalapeno peppers, chili powder, chicken stock, lime juice, and cilantro. Cook for 8 minutes. Season with salt and pepper.
3. To serve, spoon a desired amount of rice into bowls. Garnish with avocado slices.

Recipe #26 - Rainbow Seafood Marinara

Prep time – 30 minutes
Serving size – 4

Nutrition facts:
Calories – 554.5
Carbohydrates – 99.3 grams
Total Fat – 9.9 grams
Protein – 20.4 grams

Ingredients:
For the noodles
- 4 streaky bacon, thinly sliced
- 1 carrot
- 1 sweet potato
- 1 zucchini
- ¼ summer squash
- Pinch of sea salt, add more if needed
- Pinch of black pepper, to taste
- ¼ cup water

For the marinara sauce
- 1 Tbsp. olive oil
- 1 onion, minced

- 4 garlic cloves, minced
- 1 can crushed tomatoes, drained
- 2 tomatoes, minced
- 1 cup vegetable stock
- 1 Tbsp. tomato paste
- 1 tsp. oregano powder
- Dash of Spanish paprika
- 1 tsp. thyme powder
- 1 fresh jalapeno, minced
- 1 pound mussels, shells scrubbed
- 1 pound shrimps, deveined
- 1 pound small clams, soaked in brine for 1 hour
- 2 tsp. lemon juice, freshly squeezed

Directions:
1. Preheat the oven to 400°F. Line a baking sheet with parchment paper.
2. For the noodles, put the bacon in a skillet. Pour just enough water over. Bring to a boil for 10 minutes or until the liquid has evaporated.
3. When the skillet is dry, reduce the heat. Let the fat melt and for the bacon to turn crispy. Reserve the bacon grease for later.

4. Remove skillet from heat. Transfer bacon bits to a plate. Allow to cool completely.
5. Using Blade B of the spiralizer, spiralize summer squash, carrots, sweet potatoes, and zucchini into thick noodles. Set aside.
6. Pour bacon grease over the zoodles. Season with salt and pepper. Toss well to combine.
7. Transfer zoodles on a baking dish. Bake for 20 minutes.
8. Remove baking sheet out of the oven and allow zoodles to cool before using.
9. For the marinara, pour olive oil in a saucepan. Sauté garlic and onion for 3 minutes or until aromatic and translucent. Tip in fresh and canned tomatoes.
10. Pour vegetable stock, tomato paste, oregano powder, Spanish paprika powder, thyme powder, jalapeño, and lemon juice. Bring mixture to a boil.
11. Add in mussels, shrimps, and clams. Cook for 20 seconds. Turn off the heat and allow residual heat cook the seafood.
12. Transfer clams, mussels and shrimp to a bowl. Continue cooking the sauce until the liquid is reduced by half.

13. To serve, put an equal amount of zoodles on a plate. Put shrimp, clams, and mussels on top. Spoon ½ cup of marinara sauce. Garnish with bacon bits.

Recipe #27: Italian Meatball Stew with Zucchini Noodles

Prep time – 3 hours and 40 minutes
Serving size – 4

Nutrition facts:
Calories – 158.5
Carbohydrates – 16.3 grams
Total Fat – 7.2 grams
Protein – 8.1 grams

Ingredients:

For the meatballs
- 1 Tbsp. olive oil
- 1½ pound lean ground beef
- 1 egg
- 1 onion, minced
- 5 garlic cloves, minced
- 1½ tsp. onion powder
- ½ cup steel rolled oats
- 1 tsp. oregano powder
- 1 tsp. Italian seasoning

- ½ cup Parmesan cheese, grated
- 1 Tbsp. fennel fronds, minced
- Pinch of sea salt, add more if needed
- Pinch of black pepper, to taste

For the stew
- 1 zucchini
- 1 onion, quartered
- 1 carrot, chopped
- 1 potato, chopped
- 1 sweet potato, chopped
- 2 celery stalks, chopped
- 1 apple, quartered
- 2 tomatoes, quartered
- 4 cups chicken stock

Directions:
1. For the meatballs, put together lean ground beef, egg, onion, garlic, onion powder, rolled oats, oregano powder, Italian seasoning, Parmesan cheese, fennel fronds, salt, and in a large mixing bowl. Mix until are ingredients are well incorporated.
2. Line a baking sheet with parchment paper. Roll the beef mix into thick meatballs.

Allow to sit on a baking sheet for 30 minutes.
3. Pour olive oil into a skillet. Shallow fry meatballs in batches or until browned on all sides. Repeat the same procedure until all the meatballs are cooked.
4. For the stew, put together zucchini, onion, carrot, potato, sweet potato, celery stalks, apple, and tomatoes into the slow cooker. Pour in chicken stock.
5. Drop meatballs into the slow cooker. Cook stew for 3 hours on lowest setting.
6. Remove the lid and allow the stew to cool down for 10 minutes.
7. To serve, using Blade A of the spiralizer, spiralize zucchini to make long flat noodles. Put a handful of noodles in a bowl. Spoon beef stew on top.

Recipe #28 – Summer Broccoli and Carrots Slaw

Prep time – 1 hour and 15 minutes
Serving size – 4

Nutrition facts:
Calories – 231
Carbohydrates – 50 grams
Total Fat – 2 grams
Protein – 10 grams

Ingredients:
- 2 carrots, peeled
- ½ cup raisins, pre-soaked, drained
- 1 head broccoli, florets and stems separated
- ¼ cup almonds, slivered
- 1 ½ tablespoon lemon juice, freshly squeezed
- 1 cup Greek yoghurt
- ½ teaspoon garlic powder
- Pinch of salt, add more if needed
- Pinch of pepper, to taste
- 1 tablespoon mustard

Directions:

1. Using Blade C of the spiralizer, spiralize broccoli stems and carrots. Set aside
2. Divide florets into bite-sized pieces. Transfer to a salad bowl together with spiralized broccoli and carrots. Add in raisins, almonds, and lemon juice.
3. Meanwhile, in another bowl, combine the yoghurt, garlic powder, mustard, salt, pepper, and lemon juice.
4. Pour dressing over veggies. Gently toss to combine. Put the slaw inside the fridge for 1 hour before serving.

Recipe #29 - Carrot Rice and Lentil Stew

Prep time – 3 hours 15 minutes
Serving size – 6

Nutrition facts:
Calories – 201.2
Carbohydrates – 21.7 grams
Total Fat – 10.7 grams
Protein – 5.9 grams

Ingredients:
- 1 large carrot, peeled
- 2 garlic cloves, minced
- 1 red onion, chopped
- 2 cups tomatoes, diced
- 2 celery stalks, diced
- 1 tablespoon tomato paste
- 1 cup dry green lentils, rinsed
- 4 cups vegetable broth
- 1 tablespoon hot sauce
- 1 cup water
- Pinch of sea salt, add more if needed

- Pinch of ground black pepper, to taste
- 1 teaspoon cumin
- Pinch of cinnamon powder
- ½ teaspoon ground coriander
- ½ teaspoon turmeric powder
- 1 tablespoon lime juice, freshly squeezed

Directions:

1. Using Blade C of the spiralizer, spiralize carrot. Transfer to a food processor. Pulse until a grain-like consistency is achieved.
2. Meanwhile, layer garlic, onions, tomatoes, celery stalks, and lentils in a slow cooker. Add in carrot rice and tomato paste. Pour water, vegetable broth, and hot sauce. Season with salt, pepper, cumin, cinnamon, coriander, and turmeric. Cover the lid and cook on low for 3 hours undisturbed.
3. Squeeze in lime juice over the stew. Serve.

Recipe #30 – Spiralized Turnip Risotto with Broccoli Pesto

Prep time – 10 minutes
Serving size – 3

Nutrition facts:
Calories – 256
Carbohydrates – 15 grams
Total Fat – 9 grams
Protein – 18 grams

Ingredients:
For the turnip risotto
- 2 turnips, peeled

For the broccoli pesto
- 1 broccoli, cut into bit-sized florets, steamed
- 3 eggs, lightly poached, salted, for garnish
- 1 Tbsp. olive oil
- 1 garlic clove, minced
- 1½ fresh basil leaves
- 2 Tbsp. pine nuts, roasted
- 1 Tbsp. Parmesan cheese, grated

- Pinch of red pepper flakes
- Pinch of sea salt, add more if needed
- Pinch of black pepper, to taste

Directions:
1. For the turnip risotto, using Blade C of the spiralizer, spiralize turnips into thin zoodles. Transfer to a food processor. Pulse once. Place on paper towels to remove excess moisture.
2. For the broccoli pesto, put together eggs, olive oil, garlic, basil leaves, pine nuts, Parmesan cheese, red pepper flakes, salt, and pepper into the food processor. Process until smooth. Add the broccoli and pulse once.
3. To serve, toss the turnip risotto and pour broccoli pesto in a salad bowl. Ladle on plates. Top with poached egg.

Chapter 4 – Spiralizer Dinner Options

Recipe #31 – Egg Drop Soup

Prep time – 10 minutes
Serving size – 3 – 4

Nutrition facts:
Calories – 230
Carbohydrates – 4.2 grams
Total Fat – 7.9 grams
Protein – 13.1 grams

Ingredients:
- 1 egg, lightly beaten
- 1 zucchini
- 2 cups vegetable stock
- ½ cup water
- 3 Tbsp. nori flakes
- 1 Tbsp. ginger, grated

- 1 Tbsp. soy sauce
- ¾ Tbsp. extra virgin olive oil
- 2 tsp. rice vinegar
- ¼ tsp. red pepper flake
- black pepper, to taste

Directions:
1. Using Blade C of the spiralizer, spiralize zucchini into thin zoodles. Set aside.
2. For the soup: pour olive oil in a saucepan. Saute ginger until aromatic. Add in vegetable stock, soy sauce, red pepper flakes, vinegar, and water. Bring mixture to a boil.
3. Reduce the heat. Add in seaweed flakes. Pour in egg whilst stirring often for 30 seconds.
4. Turn off the heat. Season with black pepper.
5. To serve, place a few strands of zoodles in a bowl. Spoon a desired amount of out egg drop soup in the bowl.

Recipe #32 - Carrot Noodles in Miso

Prep time – 20 minutes
Serving size – 4

Nutrition facts:

Calories – 93.8

Carbohydrates – 11.5 grams

Total Fat – 4.8 grams

Protein – 3.4 grams

Ingredients:
- 3 carrots, peeled
- ¼ cup olive oil
- 1 tablespoon sesame oil
- 2 tablespoon yellow miso
- 3 tablespoons rice vinegar
- 1 tablespoon honey
- 2 teaspoons lime zest
- 2 tablespoons lime juice, freshly squeezed
- 3 cups cherry tomatoes
- 4 green onions, chopped
- Pinch of sea salt, add more if needed
- 2 teaspoons sesame seeds, toasted, for garnish

Directions:

1. Preheat the oven to 400°F. Prepare a baking sheet.
2. Using Blade C of the spiralizer, spiralize carrots into long strands. Set aside.
3. Combine olive oil, sesame oil, miso, vinegar, honey, lime zest, and lime juice in a bowl. Place an equal amount of dressing in another bowl. Add in cherry tomatoes. Toss well.
4. Place tomatoes on the baking sheet. Season with salt. Bake for 15 minutes or until roasted. Remove from the oven. Set aside.
5. Meanwhile, pour water in a saucepan. Bring mixture to a boil. Place carrot noodles in boiling water. Reduce the heat and allow to simmer for 3 minutes.
6. Transfer noodles in a bowl. Stir in roasted tomatoes, green onions, and the dressing. Sprinkle sesame seeds on top.

Recipe #33 - Herb Carrot Rice

Prep time – 15 minutes
Serving size – 2

Nutrition facts:
Calories – 84.4
Carbohydrates – 15.5 grams
Total Fat – 2.0 grams
Protein – 2.2 grams

Ingredients:
- 2 large carrots, peeled
- 1 tablespoon olive oil
- 2 garlic cloves, minced
- 1 teaspoon dried oregano flakes
- ½ cup water
- Pinch of sea salt, add more if needed
- Pinch of ground black pepper, to taste

Directions:
1. Using Blade C of the spiralizer spiralize carrot into thin noodles. Transfer to a food

processor. Pulse 3 times until a grain-like consistency is achieved.
2. Heat the olive oil in a skillet. Sauté garlic for 2 minutes or until light brown and fragrant. Put together carrot rice and oregano flakes. Season with salt and pepper. Cook for 3 minutes.
3. Pour water and cook for another 4 minutes or until the liquid is reduced. Serve.

Recipe #34 - Chicken Zucchini Noodles

Prep time – 4 hours and 10 minutes
Serving size – 4

Nutrition facts:
Calories – 218
Carbohydrates – 8 grams
Total Fat – 9 grams
Protein – 25 grams

Ingredients:
- 2 zucchinis
- 1 cup chicken stock
- 1 carrot, shredded
- 1 cup green onions, chopped
- 2 chicken breasts, boneless, skinless, halved
- 1 cup coconut milk
- 2 tablespoons nut butter
- 2 teaspoons fish sauce
- 1 tablespoon soy sauce
- 1 teaspoon cayenne pepper
- 2 teaspoons ginger, grated
- 1 teaspoon red pepper flakes

- 1 teaspoon olive oil
- 3 garlic cloves, crushed
- Pinch of sea salt, add more if needed
- Pinch of ground black pepper, to taste
- Handful cilantro, chopped

Directions:

1. Season chicken breasts with ginger, salt, pepper, and cayenne pepper. Place chicken breasts on a pan. Drizzle in olive oil. Brown each side for 2 minutes. Set aside.
2. Using Blade B of the spiralizer, spiralize zucchinis. Transfer zoodles in a bowl. Add in carrots. Toss well.
3. Pour in chicken stock, coconut milk, soy sauce, and fish sauce in a slow cooker. Add in green onions, garlic, nut butter, and pepper flakes. Mix well. Put browned chicken into the slow cooker. Tip in zucchini and carrot mixture. Cover and cook for 4 hours on low, undisturbed.
4. Transfer to a serving bowl. Garnish with cilantro on top.

Recipe #35 - Stir Fry Broccoli Zoodles and Beef Steak

Prep time – 1 hour and 30 minutes
Serving size – 2

Nutrition facts:
Calories – 206.1
Carbohydrates – 2.8 grams
Total Fat – 10.4 grams
Protein – 21.0 grams

Ingredients:

For the beef
- 2 rib eye steaks, fat trimmed
- 2 Tbsp. light soy sauce
- ¼ cup hoisin sauce
- ¼ cup lemon juice, freshly squeezed
- Pinch of red pepper flakes
- Dash of white pepper
- 1 Tbsp. olive oil

For the stir fry

- 2 broccolis with stems, sliced into bite sized florets
- 1 onion, sliced thinly
- 1 garlic clove, minced
- 1 fresh ginger, grated
- ½ tsp. corn flour
- 1 tsp. sesame oil

Directions:

1. For the beef, put the rib eye steaks in a freezer-safe bag. Pour in soy sauce, hoisin sauce, lemon juice, red pepper flakes, and white pepper. Seal the bag and remove as much air as possible.
2. Massage the steak and make sure to coat well before storing placing inside the fridge for 1 hour.
3. When ready to cook, preheat the oven to 400°F.
4. Meanwhile, pour olive oil into the skillet. Remove the steaks and reserve the rest for the stir-fry.
5. Once the oil is hot, slide the steaks and cook for 3 minutes or until lightly browned. Flip

and cook the other side for another 3 minutes.
6. Cover the skillet with aluminum foil place in the preheated oven. Bake for 20 minutes.
7. Remove the skillet from the oven and allow the steaks to sit for 10 minutes.
8. Take the steaks out of the pan. Chop steaks as thinly as possible. Set aside.
9. For the stir-fry, slice broccoli tops into bite-sized florets, reserving the stem. Using Blade B of the spiralizer, spiralize the broccoli stem.
10. Pour the marinade in another bowl and put the corn flour in it. Mix until the flour dissolves.
11. Heat oil in the same skillet and sauté onion, garlic, and ginger for 3 minutes or until limp and transparent. Add in broccoli florets. Stir-fry for 2 minutes.
12. Tip in sliced steaks, marinade-corn flour mix and zoodles. Cook for another 3 minutes or until the sauce thickens.
13. To serve, ladle an equal amount on a plate. Drizzle in sesame oil.

Recipe #36 - Mediterranean Zoodle Platter

Prep time – 1 hour
Serving size – 4

Nutrition facts:
Calories – 120
Carbohydrates – 6 grams
Total Fat – 10 grams
Protein – 2 grams

Ingredients:
- 4 zucchinis, peeled
- 5 chicken breast halves, boneless, skinless, pounded
- ¼ cup sun-dried tomatoes, chopped
- 3 bacon strips, chopped
- ¾ cup artichoke hearts, chopped
- ½ cup flat parsley, chopped
- 1 tablespoon capers
- Pinch of sea salt, add more if needed
- ½ teaspoon lemon juice, freshly squeezed

Directions:

1. Cook the bacon in a skillet for 4 minutes or until golden brown. Set aside.
2. Cook the chicken breasts for 5 minutes on each side using the bacon fat. Remove from the pan and drain on paper towels. Repeat with the remaining chicken.
3. Using Blade B of the spiralizer, spiralize zucchinis. Set aside.
4. Place the zoodles on the same skillet and cook for 5 minutes. Add in artichoke hearts, capers, and sun-dried tomatoes. Season with salt whilst continuously tossing.
5. Transfer to a plate. Scatter bacon on top Garnish with parsley. Place the chicken breasts on top of the zoodles. Squeeze in lemon juice before serving.

Recipe #37 - Beet Noodles with Mustard Glaze

Prep time – 30 minutes
Serving size – 6

Nutrition facts:
Calories – 130
Carbohydrates – 10 grams
Total Fat – 12 grams
Protein – 6 grams

Ingredients:
- 4 large beets, peeled
- 10 shallots, sliced
- ¾ cup olive oil
- 4 cups water
- ½ cup apple cider vinegar
- 2 teaspoons Dijon mustard
- 3 tablespoons maple syrup
- Pinch of salt, add more if needed
- Pinch of ground black pepper, to taste

Directions:

1. Preheat the oven to 425°F. Prepare a baking tray.
2. Drizzle in olive oil into the tray. Using Blade C of the spiralizer, spiralize beets and layer them on the baking tray. Season with salt and pepper. Drizzle in olive oil. Roast for 8 minutes.
3. Meanwhile, heat the remaining olive oil in a saucepan. Add in shallots and sauté for 4 minutes. Transfer to a plate. Set aside.
4. Pour apple cider vinegar, water, mustard, and maple. Allow the mixture to simmer mixture 12 minutes or until a thick glaze form. Once the mixture thickens, stir the glaze for 1 minute. Turn off the heat and let the glaze cool for 3 minutes.
5. Transfer beet noodles to a salad bowl. Drizzle in mustard glaze over. Toss well and serve.

Recipe #38 - Beet Rice Wrap with Pesto Sauce

Prep time – 30 minutes
Serving size – 4

Nutrition facts:
Calories – 58.5
Carbohydrates – 50.5 grams
Total Fat – 1.9 grams
Protein – 6.1 grams

Ingredients:
- 1 large beet, peeled
- Leaves from 4 lettuce heads
- 1 ½ cup lean ground turkey meat
- 2 garlic cloves, minced
- 1 red onion, minced
- ¼ cup water
- 2 tablespoons butter
- 1 teaspoon oregano flakes
- ½ teaspoon red pepper flakes
- 4 cups fresh basil leaves
- ½ cup olive oil

- ½ cup almonds
- 1 tablespoon garlic, minced
- Pinch of sea salt, add more if needed
- Pinch of pepper, to taste

Directions:
1. Using Blade C of the spiralizer, spiralize beets. Transfer to a food processor. Pulse until the zoodles turn into small grains. Set aside.
2. Process garlic, basil leaves, almonds, salt, pepper, and olive oil for 1 minute or until a smooth pesto is produced. Set aside.
3. Meanwhile, heat the butter in a skillet. Sauté garlic and onion for 3 minutes. Add in ground turkey, red pepper flakes, and oregano. Cook for 7 minutes. Pour water and allow to simmer until the liquid is reduced.
4. Fold in beet rice. Stir well. Cook for 5 minutes and the pour over the pesto sauce. Cook for another minute. Turn off the heat.
5. To serve, place a tablespoon of beet rice into a lettuce leaf. Roll like a burrito. Do the

same process for the remaining beet rice and lettuce leaf. Secure with toothpicks.

Recipe #39 - Beets and Beans Pickles

Prep time – 1 hour and 15 minutes
Serving size – 4

Nutrition facts:
Calories – 106
Carbohydrates – 25.13 grams
Total Fat – 0.25 grams
Protein – 2.43 grams

Ingredients:
- 2 beets, peeled
- 1 tablespoons olive oil
- ½ cup apple cider vinegar
- 200 grams wax beans, halved
- 2 tablespoons sugar
- 1/3 cup chives, chopped
- Pinch of sea salt, add more if needed
- 1/3 cup cottage cheese, crumbled

Directions:
1. Using Blade C of the spiralizer, spiralize beets into noodles. Trim to 3-inch strands. Set aside.

2. Pour water into the saucepan. Bring water to a boil and add in beet noodles and wax beans. Allow to boil for another 5 minutes. Transfer to a bowl filled with ice-cold water. Leave for 1 minute and then drain.
3. Pour vinegar, olive oil, vinegar, salt and sugar into the bowl filled with zoodles. Toss well until all ingredients are well incorporated. Transfer the mixture in an airtight container. Place inside the fridge for 1 hour.
4. Once ready to serve, place the beets and beans in a bowl. Pour just the right amount vinegar juice all over. Add in cheese and chives. Serve.

Recipe #40 - Curly Sweet Potato Fries

Prep time – 30 minutes
Serving size – 2

Nutrition facts:
Calories – 116.9
Carbohydrates – 16.4 grams
Total Fat – 5.4 grams
Protein – 1.2 grams

Ingredients:
- 1 sweet potato, peeled
- ½ tablespoon garlic powder
- ¼ cup Parmesan cheese, grated
- Pinch of salt, add more if needed
- Pinch of ground black pepper, to taste
- 1 tablespoon canola oil
- ¼ teaspoon parsley, chopped

Directions:
1. Preheat the oven to 425°F. Line a baking tray with parchment paper.

2. Using Blade B of the spiralizer, spiralize sweet potato Trim into 3-inch curls. Transfer to a mixing bowl. Add in Parmesan cheese, garlic powder, olive oil, salt, and pepper. Add in potato curls and make sure to coat well.
3. Lay potato fries on the baking sheet. Bake for 10 minutes then flip over. Bake the other side for 5 minutes or until golden brown.
4. Remove fries from the oven. Transfer to a serving plate. Sprinkle parsley.

Recipe #41 - Sweet Potato Noodles with Kale Pesto

Prep time – 40 minutes
Serving size – 5

Nutrition facts:
Calories – 200
Carbohydrates – 47 grams
Total Fat – 1 gram
Protein – 1 gram

Ingredients:
- 2 sweet potatoes, peeled
- 1 bunch kale leaves, stems trimmed off
- 1 cup walnuts
- 2 garlic cloves
- 2 tablespoons vegetable stock
- 2 tablespoons parsley, chopped
- ½ teaspoon red pepper flakes
- 1 tablespoon lemon juice
- Pinch of sea salt, add more if needed
- 2 tablespoons olive oil

Directions:

1. Using Blade B of the spiralizer, spiralize sweet potatoes. Set aside.
2. Meanwhile, pour water into a large sauce pan. Bring to a boil. Blanch kale leaves for 2 minutes. Drain completely. Set aside.
3. Bring the water back to a boil. Blanch sweet potato noodles for 2 minutes. Drain the noodles completely. Transfer oodles in a mixing bowl. Set aside.
4. Pour vegetable stock, olive oil, and kale, in a blender. Process for 30 seconds. Add in walnuts, lemon juice, garlic, salt, pepper flakes, and parsley. Process for another 10 seconds or until a desired consistency is achieved.
5. To serve, place sweet potato noodles in a serving plate. Pour green pesto sauce over.

Recipe #42 - Sweet Potato Wraps

Prep time – 30 minutes
Serving size – 6

Nutrition facts:
Calories – 95
Carbohydrates – 18 grams
Total Fat – 1 gram
Protein – 2 grams

Ingredients:
- 2 sweet potatoes, peeled
- 6 lean hotdogs, halved
- 2 ½ tablespoons butter, melted
- Pinch of sea salt, add more if needed

Directions:
1. Preheat the oven to 375°F. Prepare a wire rack placed over a baking sheet. Grease with butter. Set aside.
2. Using Blade C of the spiralizer, spiralize sweet potatoes into thin strands. Transfer to a bowl.

3. Sprinkle salt and 2 tablespoons of butter into the bowl. Toss mixture lightly.
4. Get half of the hotdog and wrap the sweet potato strands around it. Repeat the same procedure with the rest of the hotdogs. Do the same for the remaining hotdogs.
5. Place the hotdogs on the rack in the oven. Bake for 20 minutes. Flip to the other side and bake for another 10 minutes or until the potato wraps are golden brown. Serve.

Recipe #43 – Shredded Cabbage Bowl

Prep time – 15 minutes
Serving size – 2

Nutrition facts:
Calories – 8
Carbohydrates – 1.95 grams
Total Fat – 0.04 grams
Protein – 0.5 grams

Ingredients:
- 1 tablespoon olive oil
- 1 red onion, chopped
- 1 tablespoon garlic, minced
- Pinch of chili pepper
- 1 small cabbage head
- ¼ cup chicken stock
- 1 ½ cups canned tuna in water
- Pinch of sea salt, add more if needed
- Pinch of ground black pepper, to taste
- 1 tablespoons almonds, slivered

Directions:

1. Heat the olive oil in a pan. Sauté onion, garlic, and chili pepper for 3 minutes.
2. Using Blade A of the Spiralizer, spiralize the cabbage. Place cabbage into the pan and cook for 3 minutes.
3. Pour the chicken stock. Allow mixture to simmer for 2 minutes or until the liquid has evaporated.
4. Mix in the tuna. Season with salt and pepper. Toss mixture well.
5. To serve, transfer to individual bowls. Garnish with slivered almonds on top.

Recipe #44 - Butternut Squash and Spinach Casserole

Prep time – 1 hour and 30 minutes
Serving size – 4

Nutrition facts:
Calories – 152.5
Carbohydrates – 24.2 grams
Total Fat – 5.7 grams
Protein – 5.6 grams

Ingredients:
- 1 butternut squash, bottom sliced off, sliced into two
- 4 cups spinach leaves
- 4 sausage links, cases removed
- 4 fresh sage leaves
- 3 garlic cloves, minced
- 1 onion, chopped
- 1 egg, whisked
- ¼ teaspoon red pepper flakes
- ½ tablespoon olive oil
- Pinch of salt, add more if needed

- Pinch of pepper, to taste
- 1 ½ cups ricotta cheese
- 1 cup cheddar cheese, shredded
- 1/3 cup parmesan cheese, grated

Directions:
1. Preheat the oven to 400°F. Prepare a baking dish.
2. Meanwhile, combine egg, ricotta, and cheese in small bowl. Set aside.
3. Using Blade A of the spiralizer, spiralize butternut squash to make large slices. Set aside.
4. Heat the olive oil in a pan. Add in sage leaves making sure that the leaves do not get burnt. Transfer sage to a chopping board and mince. Set aside.
5. In the same pan, cook sausage for 7 minutes or until golden brown. Add in onion, garlic, spinach, pepper flakes, salt, and pepper. Cover the pan and cook for 3 minutes.
6. To assemble the casserole, layer squash slices at the bottom of the baking dish. Add in the spinach mixture. Put the egg and

cheese mixture on top. Put another set of squash, spinach and cheese mixture, and finally a layer of squash on top.
7. Put cheddar cheese on top of the squash layer. Cover with tin foil. Place inside the oven and bake for 45 minutes.
8. Remove tin foil. Scatter sage over the dish. Allow to cool for 3 minutes before serving.

Recipe #45 - Stir-Fry Radish Zoodles and Mushrooms

Prep time – 30 minutes
Serving size – 4 - 5

Nutrition facts:
Calories – 122
Carbohydrates – 8.78 grams
Total Fat – 6.9 grams
Protein – 7.38 grams

Ingredients:
- 1 Chinese white radish, peeled
- 8 Shiitake mushrooms, pre-soaked in water for 30 minutes stems cut off, roughly chopped
- 10 pieces snap peas, trimmed
- 3 green onions, chopped
- 2 tablespoons coconut aminos
- 2 tablespoons olive oil
- 1 teaspoon ginger, grated
- 1 teaspoon sea salt, add more if needed
- 1 teaspoon white pepper, to taste

- 1 teaspoon brown sugar

Directions:
1. Using Blade C of the spiralizer, spiralize radish. Set aside.
2. Meanwhile, heat the olive oil in a pan. Sauté green onions, ginger, mushrooms, and snap peas. Season with salt, pepper, coconut aminos, and brown sugar. Tip in spiralized veggies. Cook for 10 minutes. Transfer to a platter.
3. To serve, place an equal amount into plates.

Chapter 5 – Pasta and Salad Dishes

Recipe#46 - Radish, Beetroot, and Carrot Zoodles

Prep time –30 minutes
Serving size – 2

Nutrition facts:
Calories – 58.5
Carbohydrates – 50.5 grams
Total Fat – 1.9 grams
Protein – 6.1 grams

Ingredients:
For the dressing
- ¼ cup walnuts
- 2 Tbsp. lemon juice, freshly squeezed
- 1 tsp. Dijon mustard
- 1 garlic clove, grated
- ½ tsp. honey
- 4 Tbsp. extra virgin olive oil

- Pinch of sea salt, add more if needed
- Pinch of white pepper, to taste

For the salad
- 1 raw sugar beets
- 1 carrot
- 1 radish
- 4 slices halloumi
- 2 handfuls watercress

Directions:
1. To make the dressing, toast the walnuts in a pan until slightly brown. Allow to cool before chopping. Set aside.
2. In a mason jar, put lemon juice, Dijon mustard, garlic clove, honey, olive oil, salt, and pepper. Seal the jar and shake well. Set aside.
3. To make the salad, place watercress on a serving plate. Put inside the fridge before using.
4. Meanwhile, using Blade C of the spiralizer, spiralize radish, beetroot, and carrot into thin zoodles. Place inside the fridge and let it chill for 30 minutes.

5. In a non-stick skillet, grill halloumi slices for 3 minutes or until brown on both sides. Let cool before slicing.
6. To serve, pour just the right amount of dressing into the veggie bowl. Add in sliced halloumi and walnuts. Toss well to combine. Place the salad on the watercress. Drizzle in more dressing.

Recipe #47 – Spiralized Rutabaga Pasta with Marinara Sauce

Prep time –30 minutes
Serving size – 2 -3

Nutrition facts:
Calories – 66.3
Carbohydrates – 57.1 grams
Total Fat – 3.1 grams
Protein – 6.1 grams

Ingredients:
- 2 rutabagas, peeled, trimmed
- ½ cup white mushrooms, chopped
- 1 cup ground beef
- 2 garlic cloves, crushed
- 1 small onion, minced
- 1 ½ cup marinara sauce
- 1 teaspoon truffle oil
- 1 tablespoon parsley, chopped
- Pinch of salt, add more if needed
- Pinch of pepper, to taste

Directions:
1. In a pan, combine onions, garlic, beef, and mushrooms. Cook for 10 minutes. Pour marinara sauce. Season with salt the pepper. Allow the mixture to simmer for 20 minutes.
2. Meanwhile, using Blade B of the spiralizer, spiralize rutabagas to make spaghetti-like pasta. Transfer zoodles into a pot and fill it with water. Bring to a boil for 5 minutes.
3. Drain the zoodles and transfer to a platter. Drizzle in truffle oil. toss gently.
4. Pour the sauce over the rutabaga zoodles. Scatter parsley on top. Serve.

Recipe #48 - Green and Yellow Mango Salad

Prep time – 15 - 20 minutes
Serving size – 2

Nutrition facts:
Calories – 130.7
Carbohydrates – 15.5 grams
Total Fat – 7.2 grams
Protein – 3.6 grams

Ingredients:
For the dressing
- 1 Tbsp. fresh lime juice
- 1 Tbsp. apple cider vinegar
- 1 tsp. Dijon mustard
- ¼ tsp. fresh lime zest
- 2 Tbsp. extra virgin olive oil
- 1 Tbsp. honey
- Pinch of sea salt, add more if needed
- Pinch of white pepper, to taste

For the salad
- 1 carrot, peeled

- 1 green mango, peeled
- ¼ green papaya, peeled
- 1 zucchini, unpeeled
- 1 ripe mango, julienned
- 1 fresh jalapeno, julienned
- Handful fresh cilantro, chopped, for garnish

Directions:

1. For the dressing, in a mason jar, combine lime juice, apple cider vinegar, Dijon mustard, lime zest, olive oil, honey, salt, and pepper. Seal and shake well to combine. Set aside.
2. For the salad, using Blade C of the spiralizer, spiralize carrot, green mango, papaya, and zucchini into thin zoodles. Place in a large bowl.
3. Toss gently. Add in ripe mango and jalapeño.
4. To serve, drizzle in half of the dressing into the spiralized veggies. Toss well. Garnish with cilantro.

Recipe #49 – Sweet Potatoes and Prosciutto Pasta

Prep time – 30 minutes
Serving size – 4

Nutrition facts:
Calories – 558.4
Carbohydrates – 80.1 grams
Total Fat – 21 grams
Protein – 15.5 grams

Ingredients:
- 3 sweet potatoes, peeled
- ½ tablespoon coconut oil
- Pinch of sea salt, add more if needed
- 1 cup prosciutto, chopped
- 1 cup almonds, slivered
- 10 dates, pitted, chopped
- ½ cup cottage cheese
- 2 tablespoons water
- ½ cup Parmesan cheese, grated

Directions:
1. Using Blade C of the spiralizer, spiralize sweet potatoes to create long, thin noodles. Cut into 1.5-inch long strings. Set aside.
2. Meanwhile, heat the coconut oil in a pan. Add in zoodles. Season with salt. Cook for 7 minutes. Transfer zoodles to a plate.
3. In the same pan, cook the prosciutto for 3 minutes whilst stirring continuously. Add in the almonds, dates, cottage cheese, and water. Cook for 4 minutes or until the cheese melts. Tip in sweet potato pasta. Mix well.
4. To serve, put an equal amount of zoodles into individual plates. Scatter Parmesan cheese.

Recipe #50 - Beet Caprese Pasta

Prep time – 30 minutes
Serving size – 2

Nutrition facts:

Calories – 390.9

Carbohydrates – 51.5 grams

Total Fat – 16.9 grams

Protein – 12.4 grams

Ingredients:
- 2 beets, peeled
- 2 cups mozzarella cheese, torn
- 1 tablespoon olive oil
- 10 cherry tomatoes, halved
- 2 garlic cloves, sliced
- 2 tablespoons parsley, chopped
- Pinch of sea salt, add more if needed
- Pinch of ground black pepper, to taste

Directions:
1. Preheat the oven to 400°F. Prepare 2 baking dishes.

2. Using Blade C of the spiralizer, spiralize beets into long, thin noodles. Set aside.
3. Place tomatoes in a baking dish. Season with salt and pepper. Drizzle in olive oil over. Roast tomatoes for 15 minutes. Before the 15-minute mark ends, add in garlic.
4. In another baking dish, place beet noodles and roast for 5 minutes. Put the mozzarella pieces on top of the zoodles and roast for another 5 minutes.
5. Allow dish to cool. Get the roasted tomatoes and garlic from the oven and put on top of the zoodles. Sprinkle parsley on top. Serve.

Recipe #51 - Cucumber Pasta in White Sauce

Prep time – 30 minutes
Serving size – 2

Nutrition facts:
Calories – 481.1
Carbohydrates – 101.6 grams
Total Fat – 1.3 grams
Protein – 17.4 grams

Ingredients:
- 1 cucumber

For the béchamel
- 1 Tbsp. olive oil
- 1 Tbsp. butter, unsalted
- 1 Tbsp. all-purpose flour
- ½ cup Pecorino Romano, grated
- 1½ cup chicken stock, divided
- Dash of nutmeg
- Pinch of black pepper, to taste

Directions:

1. Using Blade B of the spiralizer, spiralize cucumber into thick zoodles. Slice into 6-inch long strands. Set aside.
2. For the béchamel, pour olive oil and butter in a saucepan. Reduce heat once the butter melts.
3. Whisk in flour and pour half of the chicken stock. Stir until the flour dissolves. Add in cheese, nutmeg, and black pepper. Cook for 5 minutes or until the sauce thickens.
4. Remove pan from the heat. Allow to cool for 3 minutes before tipping in zoodles. Toss well to combine.
5. To serve, place an equal amount of pasta into individual plates. Garnish with cheese on top.

Recipe #52 - Zucchini Lasagna

Prep time – 30 minutes
Serving size – 2

Nutrition facts:

Calories – 286.1
Carbohydrates – 24.7 grams
Total Fat – 14.9 grams
Protein – 19.0 grams

Ingredients:

- 4 fresh portabella mushrooms, sliced thickly
- 2 zucchini
- 1 egg, lightly beaten
- 1 onion, minced
- 1 garlic clove, minced
- 3 cups spaghetti sauce with 1 tsp. sugar
- 2 cups, frozen spinach, thawed, minced
- 3 cups ricotta cheese
- 3 cups buffalo mozzarella, torn
- 1¾ cups Parmesan cheese, grated, divided
- 2 Tbsp. olive oil, divided

- Pinch of sea salt, add more if needed
- 1 tsp. oregano powder
- 1 tsp. Basil powder
- Pinch of black pepper, to taste

Directions:
1. Preheat the oven to 350°F.
2. Using Blade A of the spiralizer, spiralize zucchini into long, thin zoodles. Slice to the length that fits in the baking dish. Set aside.
3. Meanwhile, combine spaghetti sauce and sugar in a bowl and place inside the microwave. Heat for 10 seconds on high. Mix. Set aside.
4. Pour one tablespoon of olive oil into the skillet. Cook mushrooms for 4 minutes or until lightly seared. Transfer to a plate.
5. Pour the remaining olive oil. Sauté onion and garlic for 3 minutes or until is limp and translucent. Add in the spinach and mushrooms. Cook for 5 minutes or until the spinach leaves are limp. Remove pan from the heat. Let cool.

6. In a bowl, put together cooked mushrooms, spinach, ¾ Romano cheese, egg, ricotta cheese, basil, oregano, and pepper.
7. To assemble, ladle ¼ portion of the spinach-mushroom mixture and pour at the bottom of the baking dish. Put zoodles for the next layer. Ladle ⅓ portion of the red sauce on top, and then another layer of zoodles.
8. Repeat steps until the baking dish is almost full. Finally, top off dish with the spinach-mushroom mix.
9. Scatter Romano cheese and bits of mozzarella.
10. Place inside the oven and bake for 45 minutes. Remove from the oven and allow to cool for 10 minutes before slicing the lasagna.

Recipe #53 – Quinoa Beets Salad

Prep time – 20 minutes
Serving size – 4

Nutrition facts:
Calories – 187.4
Carbohydrates – 28.7 grams
Total Fat – 6.5 grams
Protein – 5.0 grams

Ingredients:
- 2 beets, peeled
- 1 can corn kernels, drained
- ½ cup pinto beans, drained
- 1 cup avocado meat, diced
- ¼ cup cilantro leaves
- 1 cup quinoa, cooked
- ½ cup green bell pepper, chopped
- 8 green olives, pitted, halved
- ¼ cup cottage cheese
- 2 tablespoons lemon juice
- 1 tablespoon vinegar
- Pinch of salt, add more if needed

- Pinch of ground black pepper, to taste

Directions:

1. Using Blade C of the spiralizer, spiralize beets into noodles. Transfer to a blender and pulse until a rice-like consistency is achieved.
2. Place beet rice in a mixing bowl. Add in cooked quinoa, corn, beans, avocado, olives, cilantro, bell pepper, and cottage cheese. Squeeze in lemon juice and pour vinegar. Toss well until all ingredients are well combined.
3. Place inside the fridge for 30 minutes before serving.

Recipe #54 - Parsnip Puttanesca

Prep time – 45 minutes
Serving size – 4

Nutrition facts:
Calories – 227.6
Carbohydrates – 35.5 grams
Total Fat – 6.4 grams
Protein – 10.5 grams

Ingredients:
- 4 parsnips, peeled
- 1 cup tomatoes, diced
- 1 teaspoon tomato paste
- 3 anchovy fillets, chopped
- 1 tablespoon capers
- 3 garlic cloves, minced
- 1 onion, chopped
- 1 teaspoon red pepper flakes
- ½ cup parsley, chopped
- ½ cup water
- Pinch of sea salt, add more if needed
- Pinch of ground black pepper, to taste

- 1 tablespoon coconut oil

Directions:
1. Using Blade C of the spiralizer, spiralize parsnips into long, thin noodles.
2. Heat the coconut oil in a pan. Put zoodles and cook for 15 minutes over medium heat. Transfer the pasta in a serving platter and allow to cool.
3. On the same pan, sauté onion, garlic, and pepper flakes for 3 minutes. Mix in tomatoes, capers, tomato paste, anchovies, and water. Allow to simmer for 2 minutes.
4. Add in parsley. Season with salt and pepper. Turn off the heat.
5. Pour the puttanesca sauce over zoodles. Lightly toss. Serve.

RECIPE #55 - SAUSAGE SALAD WITH CUCUMBER AND ZUCCHINI ZOODLES

Prep time – 45 minutes
Serving size – 3 - 4

Nutrition facts:
Calories – 189.4
Carbohydrates – 9.6 grams
Total Fat – 13.5 grams
Protein – 7.9 grams

Ingredients:
- 1 tsp. olive oil
- ½ link smoked Hungarian sausage, sliced into thick disks
- ½ link regular hotdog, sliced into thick disks
- 1 tsp. sugar
- 2 Tbsp. white wine vinegar
- 1 red bell pepper, julienned
- 1 white onion, sliced thinly
- 1 Tbsp. black peppercorns
- 1 bird's eye chili, minced

- 1 zucchini, chilled
- 1 cucumber, chilled
- Pinch of sea salt, add more if needed
- ½ lemon, freshly juiced
- 2 stalks parsley, chopped, for garnish

Directions:

1. For the sausage salad, pour olive oil into a pan. Slide all sausages and hotdogs into the pan. Cook for 4 minutes or until most of the sausages curl at the edges. Remove from heat.
2. Meanwhile, in a bowl, dissolve the sugar in white wine vinegar. Add in black peppercorns. Pour mixture over to the pan.
3. Add in red bell pepper, onions, and bird's eye chili. Toss well to combine.
4. Using Blade A of the spiralizer, spiralize zucchini and cucumber into long, flat zoodles. Slice into 4-inch long strands.
5. Transfer to a bowl. Season with salt and squeeze in lemon juice.
6. To serve, place zoodles in plates. Place sausage on top. Garnish with parsley.

Recipe #56 – Spiralized Apples Salad

Prep time – 15 minutes

Serving size – 4

Nutrition facts:

Calories – 242

Carbohydrates – 15.02 grams

Total Fat – 20.59 grams

Protein – 2.06 grams

Ingredients:
- 3 red apples, cored
- 5 cups romaine lettuce leaves, chopped
- ½ cup almonds, slivered
- 1/2 cup raisins
- 2 tablespoons balsamic vinegar
- 2 tablespoons olive oil
- 2 teaspoons honey
- 1 tablespoon Dijon mustard
- Pinch of salt, add more if needed
- Pinch of pepper, to taste

Directions:
1. Using Blade C of the spiralizer, spiralize apples into short noodles. Set aside.
2. In a bowl, combine balsamic vinegar, mustard, honey, olive oil, salt and pepper. Pour over dressing in a bowl with zoodles.
3. Add apples and lettuce into the bowl. Toss well to combine. Scatter raisins and almonds over the salad. Serve.

Recipe #57 - Beet Pasta with Pumpkin Sauce

Prep time – 45 minutes
Serving size – 6

Nutrition facts:
Calories – 390.9
Carbohydrates – 51.4 grams
Total Fat – 16.9 grams
Protein – 12.4 grams

Ingredients:
- 4 beets, peeled
- ½ tablespoon olive oil
- 3 sage leaves
- ¾ cup chicken stock
- 2 garlic cloves, crushed
- ¼ cup shallots, chopped
- ½ cup pumpkin puree
- ¼ teaspoon nutmeg
- ¼ teaspoon cinnamon powder
- Pinch of chili pepper flakes

- ½ cup cashews, pre-soaked in water for 30 minutes
- 2 tablespoons freshly-chopped parsley
- Pinch of sea salt, add more if needed
- Pinch of pepper, to taste
- 1 tablespoon sesame seeds, toasted

Directions:

1. Preheat the oven to 425°F. Line a baking tray with parchment paper.
2. Using Blade C of the spiralizer, spiralize beets into noodles. Trim the pasta into 2-inch strands. Set aside.
3. Place zoodles on the baking sheet. Bake for 8 minutes.
4. Meanwhile, heat the oil in a skillet. Add in sage and cook for 30 seconds. Remove sage leaves. Set aside.
5. In the same skillet, sauté onion, garlic, and pepper flakes. cook for 2 minutes. Pour pumpkin puree. Season with salt, pepper, cinnamon, and nutmeg. Cook for 3 minutes.
6. Allow to cool for 3 minutes before transferring to a blender together with

cashew. Pour the broth. Process for 1 minute. Set aside.
7. To serve, place zoodles in individual bowls. Ladle pumpkin sauce over each bowl. Sprinkle parsley and sesame seeds on top.

Recipe #58 - Zucchini Pasta with Baked Meatballs

Prep time – 1 hour and 30 minutes
Serving size – 4

Nutrition facts:
Calories – 372.5
Carbohydrates – 30.4 grams
Total Fat – 16.7 grams
Protein – 26.6 grams

Ingredients:
- 2 zucchinis, lightly seasoned with salt
- 1 ½ cups lean ground beef
- ¼ cup oregano leaves, chopped
- Pinch of sea salt, add more if needed
- Pinch of ground black pepper, to taste
- 1 cup button mushrooms, sliced
- 5 slices bacon, chopped
- 8 garlic cloves, minced
- ½ cup basil, chopped

Directions:

1. Preheat the oven to 425°F. Line a baking tray with parchment paper.
2. Using Blade B of the spiralizer, spiralize zucchinis into long pasta. Transfer to a colander. Sprinkle with salt. Leave for 1 hour to drain. After 1 hour, rinse pasta and then drain completely.
3. Place ground beef, oregano, salt, and pepper in a bowl. Knead and form into meatballs. Place on the lined baking sheet. Bake for 15 minutes. Set aside.
4. Meanwhile, heat the oil in a pan. Cook bacon for 7 minutes. Sauté garlic and mushrooms for another 7 minutes.
5. Add zoodles and olives to the mixture. Cook for 5 minutes. Tip in basil leaves. Toss the dish for 1 minute. Remove pan from the heat.
6. To serve, place zoodles in a serving platter. Place baked meatballs on top.

Recipe #59 – Carbonara Zoodles

Prep time – 1 hour
Serving size – 3

Nutrition facts:
Calories – 491.5
Carbohydrates – 9.7 grams
Total Fat – 56 grams
Protein – 41.5 grams

Ingredients:
- 8 carrots, peeled
- 4 tablespoons coconut milk
- 1 onion, chopped
- 4 slices bacon
- 2 garlic cloves, minced
- ½ cup green peas
- 2 eggs
- ¼ cup parsley, chopped
- Pinch of ground black pepper, to taste
- Pinch of sea salt, add more if needed

Directions:

1. Using Blade C of the spiralizer, spiralize carrots. Set aside.
2. Cook bacon in a skillet for 5 minutes or until crisp. Transfer to a chopping board and chop bacon into pieces. Set aside. Reserve 1 tablespoon of bacon fat on pan.
3. Sauté onion, garlic, and zoodles, in the pan for 10 minutes. Stir continuously so as not to burn noodles. Transfer cooked zoodles to a serving plate.
4. Meanwhile, pour coconut milk into the pan. Tip in eggs. Cook the mixture for 2 minutes. Con Stir constantly. Add in green peas. Season with salt and pepper.
5. To serve, place an equal amount of zoodles into individual plates. Pour coconut sauce on top. Toss well to coat. Sprinkle chopped bacon on top.

Recipe #60 - Zucchini Ribbons Salad

Prep time – 40 minutes
Serving size – 4

Nutrition facts:

Calories – 76
Carbohydrates – 10.5 grams
Total Fat – 3.8 grams
Protein – 1.8 grams

Ingredients:

- 2 zucchinis
- ½ cup ricotta cheese
- ½ cup pitted olives, halved
- 2 garlic cloves, minced
- 2 teaspoons lemon juice
- ½ teaspoon pepper flakes
- ¼ teaspoon garlic powder
- ½ tablespoon olive oil
- Pinch of salt, add more if needed
- Pinch of pepper, to taste

Directions:

1. Using Blade A of the spiralizer, spiralize zucchini ribbons. Season with pepper. Set aside.
2. Heat the olive oil in a pan. Sauté garlic and pepper flakes. Cook for 30 seconds. Tip in zucchini ribbons. Cook for 5 minutes. Season with salt and garlic powder.
3. Transfer ribbons in a bowl. Scatter olives and ricotta cheese. Cover bowl with plastic wrap. Place inside the fridge for 30 minutes before serving.

Conclusion

I'd like to thank you and congratulate you for purchasing this book.

I hope this book was able to help you know more about the spiralizer and how it can make wonders in your meals. There are a lot of fruits and vegetables that you can turn into healthy zoodles.

Moreover, I hope this book was able to inspire you to eat healthy, organic produce that you can use for everything: from breakfast to pasta dishes.

The next step is to recreate your favorite meals using the spiralizer. Share these dishes with friends and family who will surely love to have this kitchen appliance.

Lastly, if you enjoyed reading the book, could you please take time to share your views with us by posting a review? Having a positive review from you helps the book stay on top of the ranks, so we can continue to reach those who can benefit from the information shared within the book. It'd be highly appreciated!

Thank you and good luck!

www.ingramcontent.com/pod-product-compliance
Lightning Source LLC
Chambersburg PA
CBHW052058110526
44591CB00013B/2260